NEW EDITION

LISTEN FOR IT

A Task-Based Listening Course

Jack C. Richards

Deborah Gordon

Andrew Harper

Oxford University Press

Oxford University Press
200 Madison Avenue
New York, NY 10016 USA

Walton Street
Oxford OX2 6DP England

OXFORD is a trademark of Oxford University Press

ISBN 0-19-434656-0

Library of Congress Cataloging-in-Publication Data

Richards, Jack C.
    Listen for it / Jack Richards, Deborah Gordon, Andrew Harper. —
New ed.
        p.   cm.
    ISBN 0-19434656-0
    1. English language—Textbooks for foreign speakers.
2. Listening.   I. Gordon, Deborah, 1952-   .   II. Harper, Andrew.
III. Title.
PE1128.R458   1994
428.3'4—dc20   94-6213
                                                CIP

Editor: Chris Foley
Project Editor: Talbot F. Hamlin
Field Editor: Bev Curran
Designer: Judith Schwartz
Art Buyer: Alexandra Rockafellar
Production Manager: Abram Hall

Cover design by Alan Barnett and Judith Schwartz
Cover photo illustration by Frank Miller

Illustrations by Ron Bell, David Cain, Chris Costello, Doug Jamieson, Aggie Whelan Kenny, Scott Luke, M. Chandler Martylewski, Debbie Pinkney, Ray Skibinski, David Slonim, Jeffrey Terreson, Winson Trang, Brett Wagner, and Rose Zgodzinski.

The publishers would like to thank the following for their permission to reproduce photographs:

Uniphoto; Gabe Palmer/The Stock Market; © Charles Gupton/Uniphoto; © John Turner/FPG International; Ken Lax/Stock Shop; Movie Still Archives; Stock Shop; Kalt/Zefa/H. Armstrong Roberts; Bob Daemmrich/Uniphoto; © Peter Johansky/FPG International; Camerique/ H. Armstrong Roberts; © David Young-Wolff/Photo Edit; © Blair Seitz/Photo Researchers; © G. Brad Lewis/Liaison International; Allen/Gamma-Liaison; B. Markel/Liaison; A. Bennett/ Spooner/Gamma-Liaison; Porter Gifford/Gamma-Liaison; Gamma-Liaison; Dennis Hallman/ FPG International; © Terry Qing/FPG International; FPG International; Sam Sargent/Liaison International; Wernher Krutein/Liaison International; © Tom Tracy/Stock Shop; Mauritius/ H. Armstrong Roberts; © Scott Berne/Stock Shop; © Michael Grecco/Stock Shop; © James Blank/ FPG International; Reuters/Bettmann.

Printing (last digit): 10 9 8 7 6 5 4 3 2 1

Printed in Hong Kong.

Introduction

Listen for It is an intensive course in listening skills for pre-intermediate- to intermediate-level students. It is intended for upper secondary-school students, young adults, and others who have studied some English but who lack the ability to follow conversational American English on everyday topics.

Listen for It is effective both as a listening text and as a listening–speaking text. It can be used in the classroom or in a language laboratory. The *Teacher's Guide* gives detailed information on how the book can be best adapted for particular situations.

Each of the seventeen units of the course is organized around a topic and related functions. The exercises in each unit of the book are designed to prepare the listener for listening by establishing background knowledge, by setting a purpose for listening, and by showing the learner how conversational language is used to express meaning. Follow-up speaking activities are also suggested.

Each unit contains the following sections:
1. **Starting out** provides some of the background information and language that is needed in order to understand conversations on the topics presented in the unit.
2. **Listening for it** contains several task-based listening activities related to the topic. The focus in "Listening for It" is on listening for meaning. This often requires the listener to determine his or her own or the speaker's purpose and to focus only on those parts of a conversation that are important for that purpose.
3. **Listening tactics** focuses on how conversational language expresses meaning.
4. **Trying it out** contains follow-up speaking activities.

The components of the course are:
- Student Book
- Teacher's Guide, with unit-by-unit teaching notes, a tapescript, and an answer key for the exercises
- three Cassettes
- three Compact Discs

The New Edition
The new edition of *Listen for It* retains the engaging, task-based listening activities of the first edition and also offers these new features:
- an attractive full-color design
- new art
- updated content
- clearly stated objectives at the beginning of each unit
- many new prelistening and speaking activities

Contents

5. HOW ABOUT A MOVIE?   24

Topic	Functions	Tactics
• Entertainment	• Inviting • Accepting and refusing invitations • Making plans	• Distinguishing invitations from conversational closings • Distinguishing *Yes/No* and *Choice* questions

6. TENNIS, ANYONE?   30

Topic	Functions	Tactics
• Hobbies and interests	• Talking about hobbies and interests • Making plans • Talking about frequency of activities	• Identifying speaker's attitude from intonation: interested/uninterested • Identifying speaker's basic message and responding appropriately

7. WHEN ARE YOU OPEN?   35

Topic	Functions	Tactics
• Times, days, and dates	• Inquiring and giving information about times and dates • Making appointments	• Distinguishing *Wh* and *Yes/No* questions • Identifying whether time or place is being stressed

8. WHAT ARE YOU DOING THIS WEEKEND?   40

Topic	Function	Tactics
• Weekend leisure-time activities	• Making and asking about plans	• Recognizing question tags • Distinguishing reduced forms of past and present in *Wh* questions

9. KEEPING HEALTHY 44

Topics	Functions	Tactics
• Health habits • Staying in shape	• Talking about health • Discussing how to stay healthy	• Distinguishing past and present in *Yes/No* questions • Recognizing positive and negative statements

10. LET'S GO SHOPPING 48

Topic	Functions	Tactics
• Shopping, prices, money	• Talking to salespeople • Comparing products and prices	• Distinguishing positive and negative questions • Identifying meaning from intonation • Identifying information focus in questions from stress

11. HOW DO I GET THERE? 54

Topic	Function	Tactics
• Locations of buildings	• Asking for and giving directions	• Listening for sequence markers • Distinguishing similar-sounding words

12. WHAT'S HAPPENING?   58

Topic	Function	Tactics
• Cultural and social events and activities	• Talking about dates, times, prices, and activities	• Listening for key words in a sentence • Recognizing whether a speaker is finished on the basis of intonation

13. WHAT'S THE MATTER WITH SARAH?   63

Topic	Functions	Tactics
• Health and illness	• Describing physical problems • Asking for and giving medical advice	• Distinguishing positive and negative statements • Distinguishing good and bad news • Distinguishing similar-sounding words

14. WHAT'S IT LIKE THERE?   68

Topic	Functions	Tactics
• Visiting towns and cities	• Describing climates • Describing locations of towns and cities • Comparing cities	• Listening and making inferences • Recognizing requests for information

15. CAN I LEAVE A MESSAGE? 73

Topic	Function	Tactics
• Messages	• Summarizing information	• Distinguishing *can* and *can't* • Distinguishing statement and question intonation

16. WHAT'S SHE LIKE? 78

Topic	Functions	Tactics
• People and their personalities	• Describing personalities • Comparing people	• Recognizing speaker's attitude from intonation • Distinguishing similar-sounding words

17. WHAT'S IN THE NEWS? 82

Topic	Functions	Tactics
• The news	• Talking about current events • Narrating a story	• Identifying information focus in sentences • Listening for sequence markers

Acknowledgments

The authors would like to thank the following teachers for their useful suggestions for preparing this new edition: Roger Barnard, Alan Brender, Merrill E. Brown, Jeff Cady, Karen Campbell, Marie Clapsaddle, Joud Jabri-Pickett, Kenneth Jones, Robert and Reiko Seltman, Vanessa Hardy, Lesley Garcia, Thom Hammond, Robert Hickling, A.P. Macindoe, Margaret Miller, Toshiro Nakajima, Yae Ogasawara, Steven Rudolph, and Richard Smith.

We would also like to thank our editors Chris Foley, Tab Hamlin, and Bev Curran for their skillful editorial guidance in preparing this manuscript for publication.

J.C.R.   D.G.   A.H.

UNIT

1

WHAT DO YOU DO?

Topic	Function	Tactics
• Jobs	• Describing a job	• Remembering and writing names and numbers • Recognizing professions

STARTING OUT

a. Match each occupation with one of the pictures. Write the number beside each picture.

1. bartender
2. doctor
3. actor
4. business person
5. bus driver
6. salesperson
7. flight attendant
8. waiter

A.

B.

C.

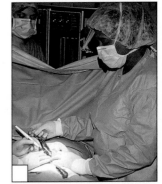

D.

E.

F.

G.

H.

b. Which of the people in the pictures do the things below? Write the number or numbers.

- [ ] work at night
- [ ] work outdoors
- [ ] wear a uniform
- [ ] need good communication skills
- [ ] travel as part of the job

LISTENING FOR IT

1a. You will hear four people telephoning about jobs. Which jobs do they talk about? Number the pictures 1 to 4.

A. [ ]

B. [ ]

C. [ ]

D. [ ]

1b. Listen again. Complete the information about each job. Check *Part-time* or *Full-time* and write in the days.

Part-time	Full-time	Days
1. ☐	☐	_____
2. ☐	☐	_____
3. ☐	☐	_____
4. ☐	☐	_____

2a. You will hear Diane, Tracy, Greg, and Joe talking about their jobs.
What does each person do? Draw a line from each person's name to his or her job.

Diane   waitress

                         businessman

Tracy
                         secretary

                         taxi driver

Greg
                         car salesman

Joe   teacher

2b. Now listen again and say if these statements are True (T) or False (F).

☐   1. Diane is not very happy with her work.

☐   2. Diane eats a lot.

☐   3. Tracy doesn't like the kind of work she does.

☐   4. Tracy likes her boss.

☐   5. Greg is not too busy at work these days.

☐   6. Greg's friend doesn't drive.

☐   7. Joe enjoys working with young people.

3. You will hear people talking about their jobs. Check (✓) below if they have the same job or a new job.

	Same job	New job
Liza	☐	☐
Tom	☐	☐
Brian	☐	☐
Kay	☐	☐
Janice	☐	☐

LISTENING TACTICS

1. You will hear people spell out their names. Write out the names below.

First name	Last name
1. _____	_____
2. _____	_____
3. _____	_____
4. _____	_____
5. _____	_____
6. _____	_____

2. You will hear people giving their telephone numbers. Write them below.

1. _____   5. _____

2. _____   6. _____

3. _____   7. _____

4. _____   8. _____

3. **You will hear people talking about jobs. Circle the job you hear.**

1. movie director   bartender   reporter

2. farmer   doctor   waiter

3. secretary   artist   actress

4. waiter   writer   doctor

5. actor   doctor   boxer

6. flight attendant   receptionist   artist

TRYING IT OUT

a. **Work in pairs. Look at the list of jobs from page 2. Which do you think are the most interesting? Number them 1 to 8 from the most to the least interesting.**

☐ bartender

☐ doctor

☐ actor

☐ business person

☐ bus driver

☐ salesperson

☐ flight attendant

☐ waiter

b. **Look at these definitions of jobs. Can you guess what the jobs are? (Answers are on page 88.)**

1. A person who tries to solve crimes and who tries to get information that will help catch a criminal.

2. A person with special training who takes care of patients in a hospital. She or he usually works with a doctor.

3. A person who draws plans for new buildings.

IT'S IN THE BAG

Topic	Functions	Tactics
• Location of objects	• Describing where things are located • Asking for help in finding things	• Recognizing prepositions in rapid speech • Distinguishing sentence and question intonation

STARTING OUT

Roger is always losing things. Work with a partner and find each thing in the picture on page 8. Write the number of each thing next to the phrase that tells where it is.

1. the cat
2. the guitar
3. the notebook

4. the dog
5. the slippers
6. the keys

7. the glasses
8. the sweater
9. the newspaper

- [ ] in the bag
- [ ] on the shelf next to the clock
- [ ] against the table
- [ ] on the floor in front of the sofa
- [ ] hanging over the chair
- [ ] behind the cushion on the sofa
- [ ] on the table in front of the radio
- [ ] between the two books on the table
- [ ] behind the curtain

A. Where's the cat?
B. It's in the bag.

LISTENING FOR IT

1. Listen to someone describing where different things are.
Put a check (✓) next to the picture that matches the description you hear.

2. Look at the pictures below. You will hear people talking about things in the pictures. Number the things in the order you hear them. The first one has been done as an example.

LISTENING TACTICS

1. You will hear a sentence containing one of the words below. Circle the word you hear.

1. on	in	6. behind	beside
2. under	over	7. under	on
3. on	in	8. beside	behind
4. under	on	9. above	in front of
5. on	in	10. in	on

2. You will hear a sentence. It will be either a statement or a question.
If it is a statement, it will sound like this:

The cat's in the shopping bag.

If it is a question, it will sound like this:

The cat's in the shopping bag?

Circle the period (.) if you hear a statement and the question mark (?) if you hear a question.

1.	.	?		5.	.	?
2.	.	?		6.	.	?
3.	.	?		7.	.	?
4.	.	?		8.	.	?

TRYING IT OUT

a. Draw a picture of a living room. Don't show anyone. Put these things in your picture:

two windows   a sofa
a coffee table   a plant
a small table   a lamp
a bookshelf   an ashtray
two chairs

b. Describe the living room you have drawn to your partner.
Your partner will listen to you and try to draw the same picture you have. He or she can ask you questions, and can ask you to repeat, but must not look at your picture.

c. Look at your partner's picture.
If anything is in the wrong place, explain where it should be.

d. When your partner has everything in the right place, change roles.
This time you listen and draw.

TALL, DARK, AND HANDSOME

Topic	Function	Tactics
• People's physical characteristics and clothes	• Describing people	• Identifying stressed words in a sentence • Distinguishing *Wh* and *Yes/No* questions

STARTING OUT

a. You have to meet these people at the airport. Work with a partner to find them in the pictures on page 13 and write the letter of the correct picture for each one.

▲ Greg Lewis. About 50, quite good looking, short gray hair, and a mustache. Usually wears a suit and tie.
Picture ☐

▲ Patricia Jordan. Mid thirties. Tall, with short blond hair. Dresses casually.
Picture ☐

▲ Bob Halpern. Early twenties. Well built. Long, dark, curly hair.
Picture ☐

▲ Diana Phillips. Teenager. Rather short and a little plump. Straight black hair. Wears glasses.
Picture ☐

A: This guy is about 50.
B: Yes, and he's quite good looking, but he's bald.

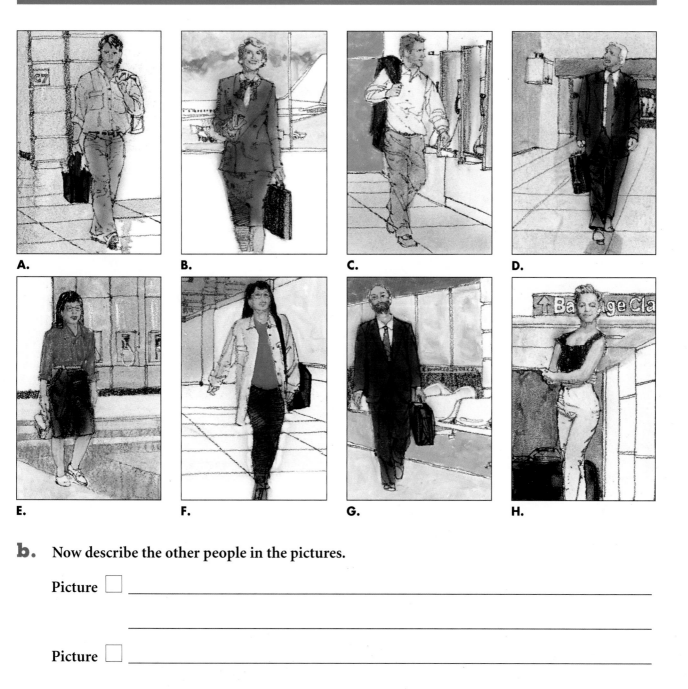

A.   B.   C.   D.

E.   F.   G.   H.

b. Now describe the other people in the pictures.

Picture ☐ _____

_____

Picture ☐ _____

_____

Picture ☐ _____

_____

Picture ☐ _____

_____

LISTENING FOR IT

1. You will hear some of the people at the party below talking
   about other guests. Who are they talking about?
   Number them in the order you hear them being talked about.

2. James Pond, Agent 006, the famous British spy, is in Rome where he has to make contact with certain people. He is listening to the descriptions of the people he has to meet. Complete his notes about each person. The first one has been started for you.

1. Agent X

Sex: _Female_

Age: _about 35_

Height: _about average_

Hair: _____

Other: _____

_____

_____

_____

2. Agent Y

Sex: _____

Age: _____

Height: _____

Hair: _____

Other: _____

_____

_____

3. Agent Z

Sex: _____

Age: _____

Height: _____

Hair: _____

Other: _____

_____

_____

4. The Boss

Sex: _____

Age: _____

Height: _____

Hair: _____

Other: _____

_____

_____

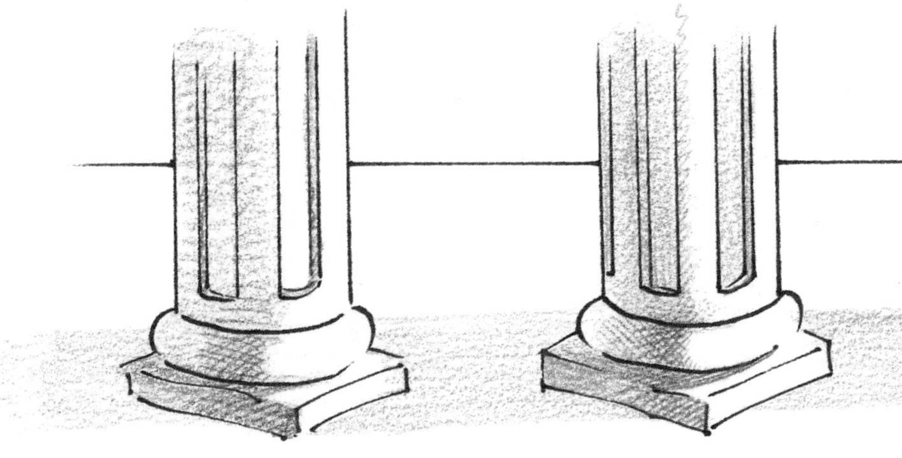

LISTENING TACTICS

1. **You will hear the sentences below. In each sentence, one word will be stressed or pronounced the loudest. Circle the word that is stressed the most. For example, if you hear:**

*She has **blond** hair,*

you circle *blond*. If you hear:

*He comes from **Boston**,*

you circle *Boston*.

1. Is he a tall guy?
2. He's shorter than I thought.
3. She has a great sense of humor.
4. Does she wear glasses?
5. That green dress is very nice.

6. He was wearing a T-shirt.
7. Why don't you wear those brown shoes?
8. Do you know Ted's brother, John?
9. That brown bag is mine.
10. That must be Beryl's husband.

2. **Circle the letter of the answer to each question you hear. For example:**

Who's that tall guy with glasses, standing near the door?

a. No, it isn't.
b. Mr. Davidson.

1. a. At the church.
   b. No, I didn't.

2. a. Yes, she is.
   b. She doesn't like bright sunshine.

3. a. Because she doesn't like cigarette smoke.
   b. No, he doesn't.

4. a. In New York.
   b. Yes, he does.

5. a. Yes, she is.
   b. John asked her to come.

6. a. Yes, he is.
   b. That's David.

7. a. Yes, he is.
   b. He has just come back from the office.

8. a. At the movie theater.
   b. Yes, I did.

TRYING IT OUT

**Work in pairs. Take turns. Describe one person in the picture to your partner.
Your partner tries to find the correct person.**

A. This person is about...
She's wearing...
She's got...hair and...

B. Is it number...?

A. No, it isn't. She's got...

HOW MUCH IS IT?

Topic	Function	Tactics
• Prices	• Talking about prices	• Understanding comparisons • Processing numbers quickly • Recognizing positive and negative statements

STARTING OUT

How much do you need for your monthly allowance? Add things to the list and give the amount you spend each month. What does your spending come to?

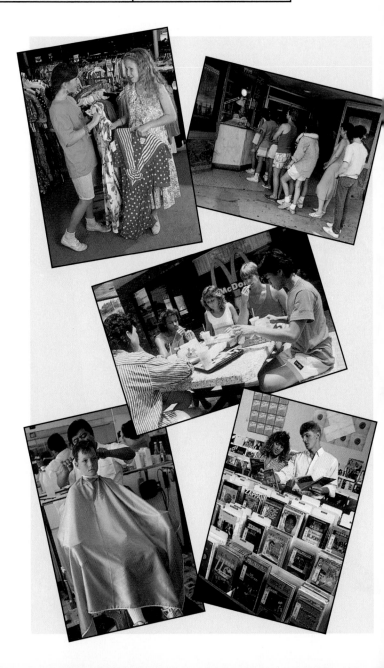

	Amount
movie	_____
concerts	_____
coffee shops	_____
restaurants	_____
transportation	_____
school supplies	_____
clothes	_____
haircuts	_____
CDs	_____
other	_____
_____	_____
_____	_____
_____	_____
	TOTAL _____

Now compare your information with others.

LISTENING FOR IT

1. This is Dee Dee's Hamburger House. Some of the prices on the menu are missing. The cashier is ringing up the prices of the things people order. Fill in the missing prices.

DEE DEE'S HAMBURGER HOUSE

BURGERS
Dee Dee Burger	_____
Double Dee Dee	_____
Cheese Dee Dee	_____
Chili Dee Dee	1.99
Double Cheese Dee Dee	_____

SIDE ORDERS
	small	large
French Fries	_____	.89
Onion Rings	.79	_____

DRINKS
	small	medium	large
Cola	_____	.79	.89
Diet Cola	_____	.79	_____
7-up	.69	_____	.89

SHAKES
Chocolate	_____
Vanilla	.89
Strawberry	.89

2a. Betty and Paul are looking for an apartment to rent. Paul is checking
through the newspaper. Which apartments does he talk about?
Circle the advertisements.

550 APARTMENTS
FOR RENT

APARTMENT FOR RENT
255 Glade Street,
2 bedrooms,
10th floor, $475
245-5433

CENTERVIEW APTS.
NEW APARTMENT
Two bedrooms,
furnished, $500
Call: **633-4434**

METCALF STREET
Quiet, 2 bedrooms,
large living/dining
room, $415
453-6373

THOMAS STREET,
near park,
1 bedroom,
large living room,
$390 **577-2344**

333 KINGWOOD
Large studio
New furnishings,
$325 **253-7390**

150 WASHINGTON AVE.
3rd floor of new
building, 2 bedrooms,
2 bathrooms $460
354-8792

UNIVERSITY AVE. AREA, 1 bedroom,
good view, $350
356-7889

TAFT RD. Near
expressway, two
bedrooms,
unfurnished $350
Call **763-3499**

2b. Now listen again. Write the name of a street beside each statement.

_____   quiet

_____   by the park

_____   too small

_____   needs furniture

3a. Mrs. Coleman is in a department store. She is asking the clerk about the prices of different things. Draw a line from each object to its correct price tag.

3b. Listen again. What does Mrs. Coleman say is wrong with everything? Write the name of each item below.

too big   _____

not the right design   _____

too heavy   _____

not the right shape   _____

3c. What is the real reason Mrs. Coleman doesn't buy these things?

LISTENING TACTICS

1. You will hear people talk about the things in each list below. Listen and circle the more expensive item.

1. red shirt   green shirt
2. Quartzon watch   Solar watch
3. black belt   blue belt
4. Multimax TV   Mitsuhashi TV
5. gray bag   red bag
6. brown shoes   black shoes
7. Singflex camera   Werner camera

2. You will hear a list of numbers. Write them down and add them up as quickly as possible. As soon as you have the answer, raise your hand.

3. In English both *Yes* and *No* can be used to agree with someone.
We use *Yes* when we are agreeing with a positive statement:

> **A:** That's a nice apartment.
> **B:** Yes.

We can use *No* when we are agreeing with a negative statement:

> **A:** That's not a very nice house.
> **B:** No.

Agree with the sentences you hear. Circle *yes* for positive statements and *no* for negative statements.

1. yes	no	6. yes	no
2. yes	no	7. yes	no
3. yes	no	8. yes	no
4. yes	no	9. yes	no
5. yes	no	10. yes	no

TRYING IT OUT

Work in pairs. You and your partner are going away to a popular vacation spot for two weeks. How much money will you need? What will you need it for? Fill in the chart, then compare your list with another student's.

Item	Money Needed
meals	

HOW ABOUT A MOVIE?

Topic	Functions	Tactics
• Entertainment	• Inviting • Accepting and refusing invitations • Making plans	• Distinguishing invitations from conversational closings • Distinguishing *Yes/No* and *Choice* questions

STARTING OUT

Do you sometimes invite a friend to do things or go somewhere with you? What do you usually do? Put a check (✓) next to things you do, then compare with others. What's your favorite thing to do?

play computer games ☐

go dancing ☐

go out for dinner ☐

see a movie ☐

go to a party ☐

go to a concert ☐

other

_____

_____

LISTENING FOR IT

1. You will hear someone inviting the people below to go somewhere.
Circle the correct diary entry for each person.

SATURDAY
movies with Ken

SUNDAY
Yankees game with Ken

FRIDAY *movies with Peter*

SATURDAY *dinner with Peter*

FRIDAY
Dinner at Pat's house
SATURDAY
Drinks at Pat's house
SUNDAY

TUESDAY
go ice skating with Fred

WEDNESDAY
go roller skating with Fred

•••••••Thursday•••••••
go dancing with Tom

•••••••• Friday ••••••••
see a concert with Tom

2a. Listen to these people accepting and refusing invitations.
Decide whether they are accepting or refusing.
Check the column under the correct response.

	Yes, thank you.	No, thanks. I can't.
1.	☐	☐
2.	☐	☐
3.	☐	☐
4.	☐	☐
5.	☐	☐
6.	☐	☐
7.	☐	☐

2b. Now listen again. Why did some of the people refuse? Write
down the numbers of the dialogues where someone refused
and their reason.

_____

_____

_____

_____

LISTENING TACTICS

1. Sometimes people end a conversation like this:

We should have lunch together sometime.

Let's get together again soon.

This is often just a way of saying good-bye. It means both people hope to get together again, but it is not really a definite invitation. Listen to these sentences and decide whether the person is really making an invitation or just ending the conversation.

	Invitation	Ending the conversation
1.	☐	☐
2.	☐	☐
3.	☐	☐
4.	☐	☐
5.	☐	☐
6.	☐	☐
7.	☐	☐
8.	☐	☐

2. We can say the following question in two different ways. If we say it like this:

Do you want me to bring a salad or a dessert?

the listener knows we want to bring something. We are asking if it is the salad or the dessert that we should bring. If we say it like this:

Do you want me to bring a salad or a dessert?

this means, "Do you want me to bring anything, for example, a salad or a dessert?" This question can be answered by Yes or No.

You will hear sentences like these. Check whether each sentence is the first type (Choose one) or the second type (Yes or No).

	Choose one	Yes or No		Choose one	Yes or No
1.	☐	☐	5.	☐	☐
2.	☐	☐	6.	☐	☐
3.	☐	☐	7.	☐	☐
4.	☐	☐	8.	☐	☐

TRYING IT OUT

The people below are inviting someone to do something. Match each of the invitations on the next page with a good response and write the letter of the response next to the invitation. Then practice the conversations with a partner.

Invitations

- ☐ How about going dancing this weekend?
- ☐ I was wondering if you might like to come over for dinner on Friday?
- ☐ What are you doing this weekend?
- ☐ Do you want to go get a drink after work?
- ☐ Would you like to go out to dinner on Saturday?
- ☐ We're having a party on Sunday; we'd love to have you join us.
- ☐ We should get together for lunch.
- ☐ Why don't we go to a disco tonight?

Accepting

a. I'd love to.
b. Great idea, let's go.
c. OK. Sounds good.
d. Oh, thank you, that'd be nice.
e. Thank you, I'd like that.
f. Oh, thank you. How nice of you to ask me.

Refusing

g. Sorry, but I've got other plans.
h. No, I can't tonight. Thanks, anyway.
i. Gee, I really can't dance.
j. I wish I could, but I'm really kind of busy right now.
k. Thanks, but I have a terrible headache.
l. I'm terribly sorry, but I've made other plans. Thanks, anyway.

TENNIS, ANYONE?

Topic	Functions	Tactics
• Hobbies and interests	• Talking about hobbies and interests • Making plans • Talking about frequency of activities	• Identifying speaker's attitude from intonation: interested/uninterested • Identifying speaker's basic message and responding appropriately

STARTING OUT

Work in pairs and find out if your partner likes doing any of the things listed below. Use phrases like those in the speech bubbles. Put a check (✓) next to the things your partner likes doing.

☐ hiking in the country   ☐ having picnics

☐ going swimming   ☐ watching baseball games

☐ going to discos   ☐ going to museums

☐ watching TV   ☐ going to concerts

What other things does your partner like doing?

LISTENING FOR IT

1. Look at the pictures below. You will hear six of these people talking
about what they like doing in their free time. What does each person
like doing? Listen to the conversations and write one of the following
names under each picture: Jan, Sam, Ted, Mary, Pat, or Jill.

1. _____

2. _____

3. _____

4. _____

5. _____

6. _____

2. Listen to this interview with the well-known scientist Lily Tarkis. What kind of lifestyle does she have? Put a check (✓) under *Always, Often, Sometimes,* or *Never* for each activity.

	Always	Often	Sometimes	Never
Get up at 5:00	☐	☐	☐	☐
Sleep late	☐	☐	☐	☐
Swim	☐	☐	☐	☐
Run	☐	☐	☐	☐
Work on the weekends	☐	☐	☐	☐
Go to the park	☐	☐	☐	☐
Relax	☐	☐	☐	☐

3. Bill and Maggie have just met for the first time at a party. They have decided that they would like to see each other again. You will hear them talking about things they like doing. What does Bill like doing? What does Maggie like doing? Write B for Bill, and write M for Maggie.

☐ going for hikes in the country

☐ going to the beach

☐ going to the swimming pool

☐ playing sports

☐ going to concerts

☐ watching Western movies

☐ watching spy movies

LISTENING TACTICS

1. Sometimes the same words can have different meanings,
depending on how they are said. For example, in answer to
> *Do you want to go to the movies?*

a person could show interest with the word:
> *OK!*

or lack of interest with the same word:
> *OK.*

Listen to these dialogues and check (✓) whether the second speaker
is interested or not very interested.

	Interested	Not interested
1.	☐	☐
2.	☐	☐
3.	☐	☐
4.	☐	☐
5.	☐	☐

2. Listen to people talking about things they like to do.
Put a check (✓) next to the best response.

1. ☐ No, not really.
   ☐ That's right.

2. ☐ Going out.
   ☐ So do I.

3. ☐ Do you really?
   ☐ Of course.

4. ☐ No, I don't.
   ☐ What day do you go?

5. ☐ I love tennis.
   ☐ That's a pity.

6. ☐ No, I get up early.
   ☐ What time do you go?

7. ☐ I do too.
   ☐ Yes, it is.

8. ☐ Not very much.
   ☐ That's right.

TRYING IT OUT

What do you think these people do on the weekends?
Work in pairs and role play the following situations.
Cover each other's information.

Student A

1. Imagine you are one of these people, but don't tell **B** who you are!
2. Change roles. Interview **B** and guess who **B** is.

Student B

1. Interview your partner about his or her weekends. Ask questions like these:

   Do you like going out?
   How do you like to relax?
   Where do you go in the evenings?

   Try to guess who **A** is.

2. Now change roles. Imagine you are one of these people.

WHEN ARE YOU OPEN?

Topic	Functions	Tactics
• Times, days, and dates	• Inquiring and giving information about times and dates • Making appointments	• Distinguishing *Wh* and *Yes/No* questions • Identifying whether time or place is being stressed

STARTING OUT

What days are these places open in your country? What hours are they open?
Complete the list with a partner, then compare with others.

	Days open	Hours
banks	_____	_____
department stores	_____	_____
museums	_____	_____
government offices	_____	_____
supermarkets	_____	_____

LISTENING FOR IT

1a. You will hear people asking for information about the places below. Listen to their conversations and write in the opening and closing hours of each place.

TRAFFIC DEPARTMENT

Monday to Friday _____

Saturday _____

Sunday _____

A.

HAY'S BOOKSTORE

Monday to Friday _____

Saturday _____

Sunday _____

B.

SCIENCE MUSEUM

Monday to Friday _____

Saturday _____

Sunday _____

C.

TOWER RECORDS

Monday to Friday _____

Saturday _____

Sunday _____

D.

1b. Now listen again. Why does each caller want to go to the place he or she calls?

1. _____

2. _____

3. _____

4. _____

2a. You will hear people calling a doctor's office to make an appointment. Listen to their conversations with the receptionist and complete the appointment cards below.

Name	
Date	Day
Time	

1.

Name	
Date	Day
Time	

2.

2b. Listen again. What is each person's problem?

1. _____

2. _____

3a. You will hear people telephoning Intercontinental Airlines to ask about flights and to make reservations. Circle the days that Intercontinental Airlines flies to each place, and also write the date that each passenger chooses.

	Days of Flights						Date of Flight

Sacramento

| Su | M | Tu | W | Th | F | Sa | _____ |

Mexico City

| Su | M | Tu | W | Th | F | Sa | _____ |

Montreal

| Su | M | Tu | W | Th | F | Sa | _____ |

3b. Listen again. Write the flight number, the departure time, and the arrival time for each passenger's flight.

	Flight #	Departs	Arrives
Sacramento	_____	_____	_____
Mexico City	_____	_____	_____
Montreal	_____	_____	_____

LISTENING TACTICS

1. Circle the letter of the answer to each question you hear.

1. a. About 9:15.
    b. Yes, I did.

2. a. Yesterday.
    b. By plane.

3. a. Yes, it is.
    b. Thank you.

4. a. At about 5:30.
    b. No, thanks.

5. a. No, you can't.
    b. By car.

6. a. Friday.
    b. Yes, I do.

7. a. On Sunday.
    b. No, I don't.

8. a. I'm not really hungry
    b. At 11:30.

2. In the following questions we can put the stress in two different places. If we say it like this:

*Are you going to the **library** on Sunday?*

the most important information is *where* you are going. Now listen to this example:

*Are you going to the library on **Sunday?***

This time the important information is *when* you are going. Listen to each question and decide if the person is asking about *where* or *when* something is happening. Check the correct answer.

	Where	When
1.	☐	☐
2.	☐	☐
3.	☐	☐
4.	☐	☐
5.	☐	☐
6.	☐	☐
7.	☐	☐
8.	☐	☐

TRYING IT OUT

Work in pairs and role play conversations like the one below. Sit back-to-back and take turns calling the places in the picture to find out when they are open. A calls B, and B gives the information A asks for. Then switch roles.

B: Evergreen Supermarket.

A: Hello, what are your hours today, please?

B: We're open weekdays from 10 A.M. to 10 P.M.

A: Are you open on weekends?

B: Saturday and Sunday from ten to six.

A: I see. Thank you.

B: Thank you for calling.

Ask your partner about the opening and closing hours of a local bank or store.

WHAT ARE YOU DOING THIS WEEKEND?

Topic	Function	Tactics
• Weekend leisure-time activities	• Making and asking about plans	• Recognizing question tags • Distinguishing reduced forms of past and present in *Wh* questions

STARTING OUT

Which of these things do you usually do on the weekend? Check the list, add other information of your own, then compare with a partner.

	Usually	Not often
do housework	☐	☐
play sports	☐	☐
go to a movie	☐	☐
go to a concert	☐	☐
watch TV	☐	☐
study	☐	☐
go to a bookstore	☐	☐
other		

_____

_____

A: Do you usually do housework on the weekend?

B: Yes, I do. How about you?

Or: No, not often.

LISTENING FOR IT

1. You will hear people discussing plans for the weekend.
Circle the letter of the phrase that describes their plans.

1. Lisa
   a. meet a friend at the pool
   b. go out on a date.
   c. go out with Cathy

2. Kim
   a. go to a movie
   b. go to a football game
   c. meet some friends

3. Kate
   a. meet friends at the airport
   b. go to a party
   c. go to Mary's house

4. Jeff
   a. study for exams
   b. meet Clint
   c. go to a movie

5. Jenny
   a. paint the kitchen with Tony
   b. paint Tony's kitchen
   c. clean up the kitchen

6. Christy
   a. stay in town
   b. visit cousins
   c. visit friends

2a. You will hear people making arrangements to do something
over the telephone. Number the correct picture.

A. ☐ _____

_____

B. ☐ _____

_____

C. ☐ _____

_____

D. ☐ _____

_____

2b. Listen again and write under each picture what they will bring and where they will meet.

LISTENING TACTICS

1. You will hear statements that can be changed into questions by adding a question tag, such as, *is he?, isn't she?, can she?,* or *doesn't she?* For example, if you hear:

> *John isn't coming to the party,*

you would choose *is he?* Listen to the sentences. Decide which one of the question tags below is correct and circle it.

1. is she?	does she?	5. will he?	does he?
2. isn't he?	is he?	6. can't it?	isn't it?
3. do they?	aren't they?	7. won't we?	aren't we?
4. is she?	can't she?	8. is she?	does she?

2. You will hear one of the sentences below. Circle the letter of the sentence you hear.

1. a. What are you doing on Saturday?
    b. What'd you do on Saturday?

2. a. Where are you going on Sunday?
    b. Where'd you go on Sunday?

3. a. Who are you going with to the movie?
    b. Who'd you go with to the movie?

4. a. When are you going to the disco?
    b. When did you go to the disco?

5. a. Why are you going to the doctor?
    b. Why'd you go to the doctor?

6. a. Who are you going to the party with?
    b. Who'd you go to the party with?

7. a. Where are you going for dinner on Friday?
    b. Where'd you go for dinner on Friday?

8. a. Where are you going fishing on Sunday?
    b. Where'd you go fishing on Sunday?

TRYING IT OUT

Write down your plans for this weekend. Write at least six things you are going to do. Then compare with a partner. How many things are the same? Who is going to have the most interesting weekend?

A: What are you doing on Saturday morning?
B: I'm going to play squash.

KEEPING HEALTHY

Topics	Functions	Tactics
• Health habits • Staying in shape	• Talking about health • Discussing how to stay healthy	• Distinguishing past and present in *Yes/No* questions • Recognizing positive and negative statements

STARTING OUT

Complete this checklist. Then compare with a partner.

   A: Do you smoke?
   B: No, never. How about you?
   A: Yes, sometimes.

Are there any habits you would like to change?

Health Information Checklist

	Often	Sometimes	Never
Smoke	☐	☐	☐
Drink coffee	☐	☐	☐
Drink soda	☐	☐	☐
Eat junk food	☐	☐	☐
Eat cake and candy	☐	☐	☐
Take vitamins	☐	☐	☐
Eat fresh fruit	☐	☐	☐
Eat fresh vegetables	☐	☐	☐
Sleep less than 8 hours a day	☐	☐	☐
Miss meals	☐	☐	☐
Play sports	☐	☐	☐
Exercise	☐	☐	☐

LISTENING FOR IT

1a. Betty and Charlene are worried about their sons Marc and Tim.
What do they think Marc and Tim should do? Fill out the chart below.

	Marc	Tim
Gain weight	☐	☐
Lose weight	☐	☐
Eat more fruit	☐	☐
Eat more meat	☐	☐
Stop smoking	☐	☐
Drink less soda	☐	☐
Start exercising	☐	☐
Relax more	☐	☐
Find a girlfriend	☐	☐

1b. How old are Marc and Tim?

2a. Helen is a reporter for a magazine. She is talking to Patty Carter, a model, about how she stays in shape. What did Helen write in her notebook? Check the things that Patty does and cross out the things she doesn't do.

Belongs to a
health club.
Gets a lot of exercise.
Uses exercise equipment.
Goes jogging.
Swims regularly.
Plays Tennis.
Eats a lot of meat.
Eats a lot of vegetables.
Smokes.
Gets enough sleep.

2b. Listen again. How many times each week does Patty exercise? Write the number next to the activities she does.

LISTENING TACTICS

1. Are these people talking about something in the past or the present? For example, if you hear:

Did you use to wear glasses?

check *Past.* If you hear:

Do you wear glasses?

check *Present.*

	Past	Present		Past	Present
1.	☐	☐	6.	☐	☐
2.	☐	☐	7.	☐	☐
3.	☐	☐	8.	☐	☐
4.	☐	☐	9.	☐	☐
5.	☐	☐	10.	☐	☐

2. Listen to people talking about sports and exercise. Is each person talking about something he or she does, or something he or she doesn't do?

	Does	Doesn't			Does	Doesn't
1.	☐	☐		5.	☐	☐
2.	☐	☐		6.	☐	☐
3.	☐	☐		7.	☐	☐
4.	☐	☐		8.	☐	☐

TRYING IT OUT

Work in pairs. How often do you do the things below? Use phrases from the box in your answer.

- never
- every day
- about once a week
- twice a month
- three times a year

How often do you...

do calisthenics?
play a sport?
take a long walk?
play golf?
swim?
go skiing?

What other exercise do you get?

LET'S GO SHOPPING

Topic	Functions	Tactics
• Shopping, prices, money	• Talking to salespeople • Comparing products and prices	• Distinguishing positive and negative questions • Identifying meaning from intonation • Identifying information focus in questions from stress

STARTING OUT

a. These pictures show different ways you can pay for things.
Write the number of each picture next to its name.

☐ cash

☐ credit card

☐ traveler's check

☐ personal check

1.

3.

2.

4.

b. Draw a line between each situation and a good way of paying.

buying a new car   personal check

buying a hamburger   traveler's checks

getting cash in a foreign country   credit card

going out to dinner   cash

LISTENING FOR IT

1. Listen to these conversations. How do people pay for the things they buy?
Check the correct answer.

	Credit card	Traveler's check	Personal check	Cash
1.	☐	☐	☐	☐
2.	☐	☐	☐	☐
3.	☐	☐	☐	☐
4.	☐	☐	☐	☐
5.	☐	☐	☐	☐

2a. A salesman is helping Terry to buy a tape recorder. He doesn't like some of the tape
recorders he is shown. What is wrong with them? What does Terry say about each
tape recorder? Draw a line from each tape recorder to what he says about it.

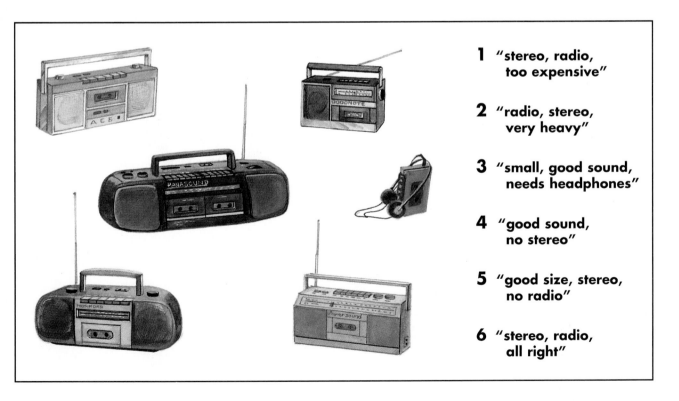

1 "stereo, radio,
    too expensive"

2 "radio, stereo,
    very heavy"

3 "small, good sound,
    needs headphones"

4 "good sound,
    no stereo"

5 "good size, stereo,
    no radio"

6 "stereo, radio,
    all right"

2b. Does Terry leave the store with his new tape recorder?

3a. Carol and Suzie are roommates. They are looking at advertisements for three different supermarkets: Tableland, Wonderfood, and Jordan's. They are comparing prices for things they need to buy. Check which supermarket is the cheapest for each item on their shopping list.

	Tableland	Jordan's	Wonderfood
eggs	☐	☐	☐
ice cream	☐	☐	☐
bread	☐	☐	☐
chicken	☐	☐	☐
apples	☐	☐	☐

3b. Now listen again. What is the cheapest price for each item?

LISTENING TACTICS

1. We can say either *I think so* or *I don't think so* when agreeing to questions.
When the question is affirmative, we usually say, *I think so.* For example:

> **A:** You are going shopping soon, aren't you?
> **B:** I think so.

When the question is negative, we say, *I don't think so.* For example:

> **A:** You aren't going shopping soon, are you?
> **B:** I don't think so.

Listen to each question and place a check (✓) under the response
that shows agreement.

	I think so.	I don't think so.		I think so.	I don't think so.
1.	☐	☐	5.	☐	☐
2.	☐	☐	6.	☐	☐
3.	☐	☐	7.	☐	☐
4.	☐	☐	8.	☐	☐

2. Listen to this statement.

That's $14.40, please.

You can reply to this statement in two ways. If you are *not sure* what the speaker said, you will need to check the price, so you reply like this:

Fourteen forty?

But to show that you do understand, you reply like this:

Fourteen forty.

Now listen to these conversations. Is the second speaker checking the number, or showing that he or she understands?

Checking	Understands
1. ☐	☐
2. ☐	☐
3. ☐	☐
4. ☐	☐
5. ☐	☐
6. ☐	☐
7. ☐	☐

3. These three speakers are all checking that they have heard the price *$3.55* correctly. What part of the price are they checking?

***Three** fifty-five?*

This speaker is not sure if the price is *three* fifty-five or six fifty-five.

*Three **fifty**-five?*

This speaker is not sure if the price is three *fifty*-five or maybe three sixty-five.

*Three fifty-**five**?*

This speaker is not sure if the price is three fifty-*five*, or maybe three fifty-*three*.

Circle below the part of the number that each of these speakers is checking.

1. two   seventy-one

2. thirteen   forty-two

3. nineteen   seventy-five

4. two   twenty-eight

5. thirty-two   twenty-seven

6. six   fifty-four

7. seventeen   thirty-six

TRYING IT OUT

Work in pairs and role play this situation. Cover each other's information.

Student A
You go to a department store to buy a new watch. You don't want to spend more than $50. You want a digital watch that shows the time and the date. It must be waterproof and the strap must be made of either leather or plastic. Choose one of the watches the salesperson shows you. Decide how you want to pay.

Student B
You are a salesperson in the watch department of a department store. Your department has a sale on watches this week. Find out what kind of watch the customer wants. Describe some of the watches you have on sale. Find out how the customer wants to pay.

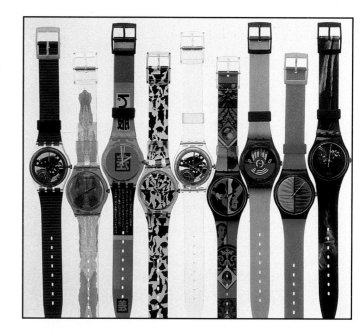

HOW DO I GET THERE?

Topic	Function	Tactics
• Locations of buildings	• Asking for and giving directions	• Listening for sequence markers • Distinguishing similar-sounding words

STARTING OUT

Read these directions and write the correct number for each place on the map, then compare with a partner.

1. bank
2. bookstore
3. post office
4. hotel
5. restaurant
6. music store

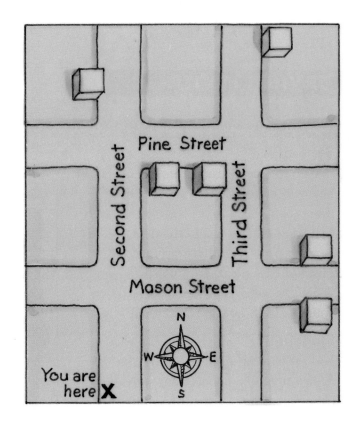

a. Go straight up Second and take the second street on your right. The bank (1) is just around the corner on the right.

b. Go up Second to Mason. Go east down Mason. Cross Third. The bookstore (2) is near the end on the left, opposite the post office (3).

c. The hotel (4) is on the corner of Third and Pine, on the right-hand side.

d. The restaurant (5) is about two blocks from here on Second. It's just past the intersection of Second and Pine on the left-hand side.

e. The music store (6) is on Third, down the end on the right.

LISTENING FOR IT

1. Look at this picture of River Street. A visitor is asking questions about the places listed below. Mark each place A, B, C, D, or E on the picture.

A. bus station   **D.** parking lot

B. subway entrance   **E.** taxi stand

C. Department of Immigration

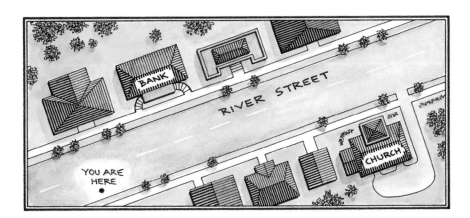

2a. Look at the map. You are standing at the corner of Wilson Avenue and Sixth Street, facing east. You will hear three sets of directions. Circle the place you will arrive at if you follow these directions.

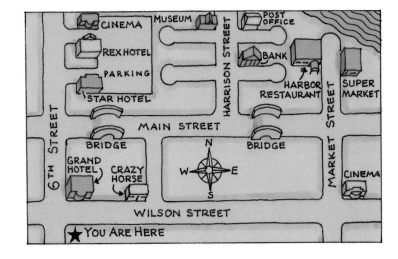

2b. Now write the name of each place below.

1. _____

2. _____

3. _____

LISTENING TACTICS

1. You will hear directions that mention two things or places. Write *1* in the box next to the first thing you will see and *2* in the box next to the second thing you will see. For example:

Before you cross the bridge, you'll see a bank.

    1 bank   **2** bridge

1.   ☐ supermarket   ☐ bridge
2.   ☐ park   ☐ museum
3.   ☐ hotel   ☐ road
4.   ☐ corner   ☐ theater
5.   ☐ shopping center   ☐ theater
6.   ☐ hospital   ☐ intersection
7.   ☐ traffic lights   ☐ bridge

2. You will hear one of the sentences below. Circle the letter of the sentence you hear.

1.   a. It's the building next to the bank.
     b. It's the building near the bank.

2.   a. It's two blocks past Smith Street.
     b. It's two blocks from Smith Street.

3.   a. It's the first street on the right.
     b. It's the third street on the right.

4.   a. It's not far after the bridge.
     b. It's not as far as the bridge.

5.   a. Take Dole up to 41st Street.
     b. Take Dole after 41st Street.

6.   a. It's just after the bank next to the station.
     b. It's just opposite the bank next to the station.

7.   a. There's a post office a few blocks down on the left.
     b. There's a post office five blocks down on the left.

TRYING IT OUT

Work in pairs. Take turns with your partner giving directions to the places below. Then compare with others.

1. from the bank to the hotel
2. from the museum to the post office
3. from the school to the library
4. from the restaurant to the coffee shop

> **A:** How do you get from the bank to the hotel?
> **B:** Well, you turn left when you come out of the bank and go along...

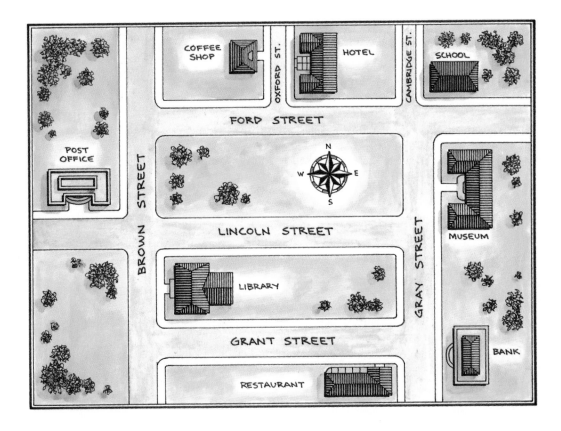

WHAT'S HAPPENING?

Topic	Function	Tactics
• Cultural and social events and activities	• Talking about dates, times, prices, and activities	• Listening for key words in a sentence • Recognizing whether a speaker is finished on the basis of intonation

STARTING OUT

Have you done any of the things below in the last two months?
Complete the chart, then compare with a partner.

	Yes	No		Yes	No
been to a movie	☐	☐	been to a museum or art gallery	☐	☐
watched a live sport	☐	☐	taken someone out for dinner	☐	☐
been to a concert	☐	☐	been to a party	☐	☐
been to a disco	☐	☐			

LISTENING FOR IT

1a. You will hear six short conversations. Where are the speakers?
Write the number of the conversation in the first box under each picture.

A. ☐ ☐

B. ☐ ☐

C. ☐ ☐

D. ☐ ☐

E. ☐ ☐

F. ☐ ☐

1b. Listen again and decide if the people like the activity or place. Put a check (✓) in the second box under the picture if they like it. Put an (✗) if they do not like it.

2a. You will hear four radio announcements. As you listen, find the picture that matches the announcement, and write the day or days when the event will take place.

A. ☐   Days _____

Time_____

Price_____

B. ☐   Days _____

Time_____

Price_____

C. ☐   Days _____

Time_____

Price_____

D. ☐   Days _____

Time_____

Price_____

2b. Now listen again, and write the time of each event and the price of admission on the lines above.

LISTENING TACTICS

1. You will hear sentences with the words below. Number the words 1, 2, and 3
in the order in which you hear them. For example:

The *movie starts* at *six* this evening.

$\boxed{3}$ six $\boxed{1}$ movie $\boxed{2}$ starts

1. ☐ Saturday   ☐ football   ☐ Sunday
2. ☐ exciting   ☐ really   ☐ concert
3. ☐ Wednesday   ☐ fireworks   ☐ don't
4. ☐ disco   ☐ noisy   ☐ much
5. ☐ keep   ☐ this   ☐ win
6. ☐ don't   ☐ want   ☐ here
7. ☐ prepare   ☐ easy   ☐ pie
8. ☐ say   ☐ started   ☐ what

2. It is possible to say the following sentence in two ways. If the speaker says it like this:

There will be dancing and singing and games!

he *has* finished what he wants to say. If he says it like this:

There will be dancing and singing and games...

he *has not* finished what he wants to say. He wishes to continue.

You will hear a number of statements. If you think the speaker has finished the
statement, check *Finished*. If you think the speaker wishes to continue speaking,
check *Not finished*.

	Finished	Not finished		Finished	Not finished
1.	☐	☐	5.	☐	☐
2.	☐	☐	6.	☐	☐
3.	☐	☐	7.	☐	☐
4.	☐	☐	8.	☐	☐

TRYING IT OUT

**Work in pairs. Put the sentences in order to make a conversation.
Then take turns inviting your partner to one of the events below.
Choose a time and a place to meet.**

☐   Can we meet at...?

☐   Sure. What's on?

☐   Sounds good. What time do you want to meet?

☐   Would you like to go to...this weekend?

☐   Why don't we meet at...?

☐   Great. I'll see you on...

☐   OK. And where do you want to meet?

☐   ...is on at...

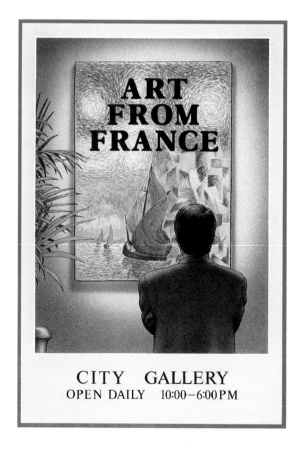

WHAT'S THE MATTER WITH SARAH?

Topic	Functions	Tactics
• Health and illness	• Describing physical problems • Asking for and giving medical advice	• Distinguishing positive and negative statements • Distinguishing good and bad news • Distinguishing similar-sounding words

STARTING OUT

a. Work in pairs and match each of these medical problems with a picture.

1. stomachache
2. cold
3. sprained ankle
4. headache
5. broken leg
6. black eye
7. fever
8. sore throat

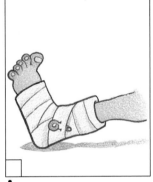

A.

B.

C.

D.

E.

F.

G.

H.

b. Talk about the people with the above problems
with your partner. For example:

> **A:** What's the matter with him?
> **B:** He has a headache.

LISTENING FOR IT

1a. This has been a bad week for Sarah! What are her problems?
Mark each problem with an (✗).

1b. Listen again. Write the day when each problem began.

_____

1c. Why don't Sarah's friends want to listen to her?

_____

2. Kevin is at the doctor's. He has the flu. Look at the pictures below, then listen to the conversation. What does the doctor tell Kevin to do? Circle the correct picture.

1.

2.

3.

4.

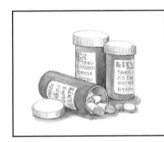 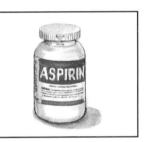

5.

3. Listen to the conversations and decide where each conversation is taking place. Number the pictures from 1 to 6.

LISTENING TACTICS

1. We can say *me too* or *me neither* when we want to respond to a statement that we feel the same way about. We use *me too* if the statement is positive. For example:

> **A:** I'm feeling sick today.
> **B:** Me too.

We use *me neither* when the statement is negative. For example:

> **A:** I don't feel well today.
> **B:** Me neither.

Agree with the statements you will hear. Circle *me too* if the statement is positive. Circle *me neither* if the statement is negative.

1. me too	me neither	6. me too	me neither
2. me too	me neither	7. me too	me neither
3. me too	me neither	8. me too	me neither
4. me too	me neither	9. me too	me neither
5. me too	me neither	10. me too	me neither

2. Check the best response to each statement you hear.

I'm sorry to hear that	I'm glad to hear that

1. ☐ ☐
2. ☐ ☐
3. ☐ ☐
4. ☐ ☐
5. ☐ ☐
6. ☐ ☐
7. ☐ ☐
8. ☐ ☐

3. You will hear one of the sentences below.
Circle the letter of the sentence that you hear.

1.   a. Take a teaspoon after breakfast.
     b. Take a teaspoon and a half at breakfast.

2.   a. Take half a teaspoon in the morning.
     b. Take a teaspoon and a half in the morning.

3.   a. Take two teaspoons three times a day with meals.
     b. Take two teaspoons three times a day before meals.

4.   a. Take these pills with meals.
     b. Take three pills with meals.

5.   a. Take three teaspoons in the morning.
     b. Take three tablespoons in the morning.

6.   a. Use this cream when it hurts.
     b. Use this cream where it hurts.

7.   a. Take one teaspoon three times a day.
     b. Take one teaspoon three times today.

TRYING IT OUT

Work in pairs and decide what remedies you would
suggest for people with each problem.
Give suggestions, then compare around the class.

Problems	Remedies
■ a headache	■ take vitamin C
■ backache	■ take some pills
■ a sore throat	■ stay in bed
■ a bad cold	■ call the doctor
■ a hangover	■ drink lots of liquids
■ upset stomach	■ drink hot tea

A: For a headache I usually...
B: Yeah, that's good. You can also...

WHAT'S IT LIKE THERE?

Topic	Functions	Tactics
• Visiting towns and cities	• Describing climates • Describing locations of towns and cities • Comparing cities	• Listening and making inferences • Recognizing requests for information

STARTING OUT

New York is cool and rainy in the spring, hot in the summer, cool in the fall, and cold in the winter. What is the weather like in your hometown? Fill in the table.

<table>
<tr><td></td><td>New York</td><td>Your hometown</td></tr>
<tr><td>Spring</td><td>_____</td><td>_____</td></tr>
<tr><td>Summer</td><td>_____</td><td>_____</td></tr>
<tr><td>Fall</td><td>_____</td><td>_____</td></tr>
<tr><td>Winter</td><td>_____</td><td>_____</td></tr>
</table>

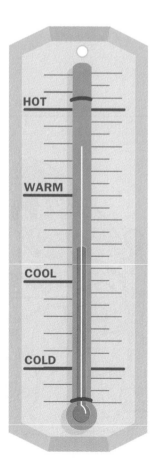

HOT

WARM

COOL

COLD

BEACH

LISTENING FOR IT

1a. Jose is a taxi driver in San Francisco, and he often meets people from faraway places. In the conversations you will hear, Jose is talking to people about the climate in Honolulu, San Francisco, Cairo, and Melbourne. Fill in the table, showing what he learns about these cities.

	Honolulu	San Francisco	Cairo	Melbourne
Jan.				
Feb.				
Mar.				
Apr.				
May				
June				
July				
Aug.				
Sept.				
Oct.				
Nov.				
Dec.				

1b. Listen again. When is the best time to visit each place? Mark the best month(s) with a check (✓).

1c. What do you think the weather is like in these places at other times of the year? Talk with a classmate.

2a. Jack White is on vacation. He has just arrived at a hotel in a small town called Oakville. He is talking to the hotel receptionist about the towns below. Mark on the map where each town is.

1. Norwalk   4. Greenville
2. Amitsville   5. Westview
3. Newton   6. Graytown

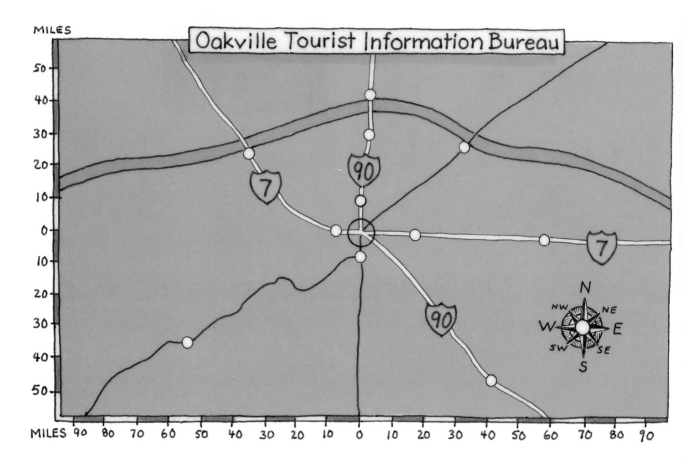

2b. Listen again and answer these questions.

Where is the museum? _____

Where do Jack's friends live? _____

Where can you take a boat ride? _____

Where are the old houses? _____

Which city does Jack decide not to visit? _____

LISTENING TACTICS

1. Listen to people talking about their hometowns and circle if the statements below are True (T) or False (F).

1. The town is an interesting place to visit.   T   F

2. The summer's the best time to visit.   T   F

3. It's a good place to go shopping.   T   F

4. There are lots of interesting things to do there.   T   F

5. It's a safe place to visit.   T   F

6. It's a long way from the sea.   T   F

7. It's a popular place for tourists.   T   F

8. It's an interesting old town.   T   F

2. You will hear people giving information to someone about places. Does the second speaker ask for more information or not? Check the correct column below.

	Needs more information	Doesn't need more
1.	☐	☐
2.	☐	☐
3.	☐	☐
4.	☐	☐
5.	☐	☐
6.	☐	☐

TRYING IT OUT

Work in pairs. Two visitors from another country are planning to spend a few days in your town or city. What should they do? Draw up a program of at least six things they should do and see. For example, they could visit a famous church or temple, buy some handicrafts, or attend a street festival. Then compare around the class.

A: What are some interesting things they should do?
B: Well, I think they should...

Suggestions

1. _____

2. _____

3. _____

4. _____

5. _____

6. _____

CAN I LEAVE A MESSAGE?

Topic	Function	Tactics
• Messages	• Summarizing information	• Distinguishing *can* and *can't* • Distinguishing statement and question intonation

STARTING OUT

Work in pairs. Look at these messages. Who do you think wrote them? Write your answers under the messages. More than one answer is possible for each message.

I'm going to a school basketball game this evening, so I'll be home late. Don't make any dinner for me.
Love,
Billy

It's my birthday on Saturday! Can you come to a party at my house? How about bringing some music for dancing?

Could you pick up some chicken at the supermarket on your way home from work?
Love,
Jane

MEMO:

Could you please meet Bob Salem, a client from New York, arriving on UA 65 at 4:15, and take him to the Plaza Hotel?

F.R.M.

1. _____

2. _____

3. _____

4. _____

LISTENING FOR IT

1a. Marcy has a telephone answering machine. She's not at home and has asked her roommate, Ellen, to listen to her messages. Listen to each message on the machine. Then check the note that Ellen wrote. Cross out any parts of each note that are incorrect.

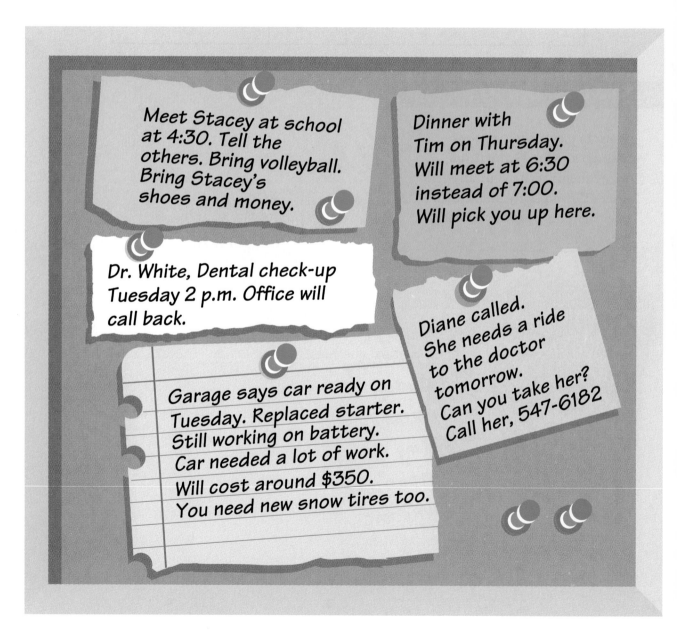

Meet Stacey at school at 4:30. Tell the others. Bring volleyball. Bring Stacey's shoes and money.

Dinner with Tim on Thursday. Will meet at 6:30 instead of 7:00. Will pick you up here.

Dr. White, Dental check-up Tuesday 2 p.m. Office will call back.

Garage says car ready on Tuesday. Replaced starter. Still working on battery. Car needed a lot of work. Will cost around $350. You need new snow tires too.

Diane called. She needs a ride to the doctor tomorrow. Can you take her? Call her, 547-6182

1b. Listen again and correct each note.

2. Listen to this receptionist taking messages. She works at the famous Fame and Fortune Talent Agency in Hollywood. Complete the information.

WHILE YOU WERE OUT

To:

From:

Company:

Phone number:

Message:

Telephoned	Returned your call	Will call again
☐	☐	
Wants to see you:	Please call back:	Came in
☐	☐	

WHILE YOU WERE OUT

To:

From:

Company:

Phone number:

Message:

Telephoned	Returned your call	Will call again
☐	☐	☐
Wants to see you:	Please call back:	Came in:
☐	☐	☐

WHILE YOU WERE O

To:

From:

Company:

Phone number:

Message:

Telephoned	Returned your call	Will call again
☐	☐	☐
nts to you:	Please call back:	Came in:
☐	☐	☐

LISTENING TACTICS

1. Notice the difference in pronunciation between these two sentences:

I can meet you on Monday.
I can't meet you on Monday.

You will hear statements about things that *can* and *can't* be done. If you hear:

You can't park your car here,

you circle *can't*. If you hear:

You can park your car here,

you circle *can*.

1. can	can't	6. can	can't
2. can	can't	7. can	can't
3. can	can't	8. can	can't
4. can	can't	9. can	can't
5. can	can't	10. can	can't

2. You will hear a sentence. It will be either a statement or a question. Circle the period (.) if you hear a statement, or the question mark (?) if you hear a question.

1.	.	?	6.	.	?
2.	.	?	7.	.	?
3.	.	?	8.	.	?
4.	.	?	9.	.	?
5.	.	?	10.	.	?

TRYING IT OUT

Work in pairs and role play these situations. Cover each other's information.

Student A

1. You are the receptionist at a hotel. A telephone caller wants to speak to Mrs. Roberts, a guest in the hotel.
   ▲ Tell the caller that Mrs. Roberts is not in her room.
   ▲ Ask if the caller would like to leave a message.
   ▲ Take down the message.

You start. Begin like this:

Garden Hotel. Reception.

2. While traveling on a bus, you found a large envelope addressed to a Mr. Ted Miller at the Garden Hotel.
    ▲ Call the hotel to inform Mr. Miller.
    ▲ If he is not in, leave a message saying what happened.
    ▲ Tell Mr. Miller where and when he can get the envelope from you.

Your partner starts.

Student B

1. You want to speak to a friend, Mrs. Roberts, who is staying at a local hotel.
    ▲ Call the hotel.
    ▲ If she is not in, leave her a message to call you when she gets back.
      Give the necessary information.

Your partner starts.

2. You are the hotel receptionist. A caller wants to speak to Mr. Ted Miller. He is not in.
    ▲ Ask if the caller wants to leave a message.
    ▲ Take down the caller's message.

You start.

WHAT'S SHE LIKE?

Topic	Functions	Tactics
• People and their personalities	• Describing personalities • Comparing people	• Recognizing speaker's attitude from intonation • Distinguishing similar-sounding words

STARTING OUT

Look at the jobs listed. What qualities do you need for each job? Work in pairs. Choose phrases from the lists and add others of your own. Form sentences like these to help you decide which qualities are needed for the jobs.

> A *waiter* has to be *organized.*
> An *actor* has to have *a good speaking voice.*

Job	Quality
waiter/waitress	(be) good-looking
teacher	organized
tour guide	intelligent/smart/bright
secretary	well dressed
athlete	serious
receptionist	friendly
politician	easy to get along with
	(have) a good speaking voice
	a good personality
	a good memory

LISTENING FOR IT

1a. You will hear four people talking about their families.
Choose the picture that matches each description.
Label the correct picture with the speaker's name: Tim, Mary, Jane, or David.

A. _____

B. _____

C. _____

D. _____

1b. Listen again and answer these questions.

1. Who plays the piano?_____

2. Who loves animals? _____

3. Who ran in a marathon? _____

4. Who is a nurse? _____

2a. Mr. Day and Ms Mendoza work in a hotel. Today they interviewed four people for the job of hotel receptionist. They are talking about each person. Mark what they liked (✓) or did not like (✗) about each person.

	Intelligence	Appearance	Personality	Voice
Frank	☐	☐	☐	☐
Barbara	☐	☐	☐	☐
David	☐	☐	☐	☐
Lois	☐	☐	☐	☐

2b. Look again at your chart. Who do you think got the job?

LISTENING TACTICS

1. Listen to this conversation.

> **A:** Do you like Bill?
> **B:** Mmm!

Speaker B likes Bill a lot. Now listen to this conversation.

> **A:** Do you like Fred?
> **C:** Mmm.

Speaker C does not like Fred very much. Listen to these conversations and decide if the second speaker likes what A asks about. Check *Likes* or *Doesn't like*.

	Likes	Doesn't like
1.	☐	☐
2.	☐	☐
3.	☐	☐
4.	☐	☐
5.	☐	☐
6.	☐	☐
7.	☐	☐

2. You will hear sentences containing one of the words in each pair below.
Circle the word you hear.

1. impolite   polite
2. uncomfortable   comfortable
3. unpleasant   pleasant
4. unhealthy   healthy
5. unintelligent   intelligent
6. unimportant   important
7. impossible   possible
8. unhappy   happy
9. unfriendly   friendly

TRYING IT OUT

Work in pairs. Talk about each other's families.
Ask these questions and others of your own.

1. How many are there in your family?
2. How old are they?
3. What do they do?
4. What are they good at? What aren't they good at?
5. Are you most like your father or your mother? Why?
6. What hobbies do they have?
7. Do you have any pets in your family?

WHAT'S IN THE NEWS?

Topic	Functions	Tactics
• The news	• Talking about current events • Narrating a story	• Identifying information focus in sentences • Listening for sequence markers

STARTING OUT

Work with a partner. Look at the beginnings of headlines for newspaper stories. Can you complete them? Compare your suggestions around the class.

Dollar Continues to

Mail Carriers Threaten

Space Shuttle

Computer Hacker Imprisoned for

Fire Fighters Try

LISTENING FOR IT

1a. Listen to the news program. Draw a line between a newspaper headline and the place where the story happened.

Place	Headline
New York	Postal Service Makes Agreement with Nudists
Washington	Fire Fighters Try to Save Homes in California Forest
Florida	Value of Dollar Falls, But Yen Rises
California	Teenagers Arrested for Computer Crimes
New Jersey	Space Shuttle Delayed
Ohio	Better Security on International Flights

1b. Read these statements. Listen to the news program again and say if the statements are True (T) or False (F).

☐ 1. There was a small fire near San Francisco.

☐ 2. Poisonous plants are a problem for fire fighters.

☐ 3. Better security is needed on airplanes.

☐ 4. There will not be armed security personnel on international airplanes.

☐ 5. The space shuttle will take off on Tuesday.

☐ 6. The boys used their computers to make telephone calls.

☐ 7. The boys were selling secrets to the Russians.

☐ 8. The dollar has risen in value.

☐ 9. The dollar is worth 98 yen today.

☐ 10. The nudists have not received mail for over a year.

☐ 11. The nudists must stay inside when the mail comes.

2a. Look at these police drawings of a bank robbery. Listen to the news
report and then number the pictures 1 to 6 in the order you hear them.

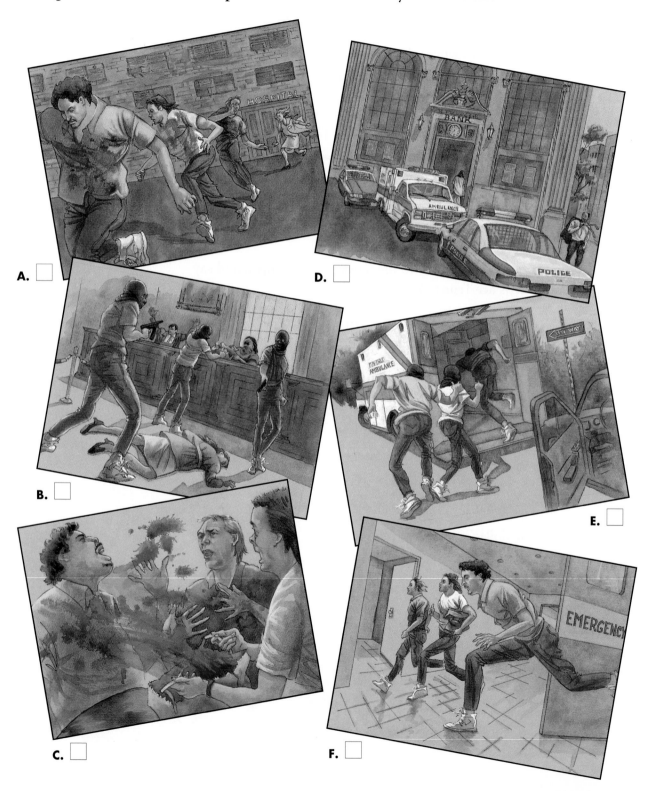

A.

B.

C.

D.

E.

F.

2b. Listen to the news report again. Work in pairs and role play this situation.

Student A
You are a TV interviewer. You are interviewing someone involved in the robbery. Find out who the person is and ask him or her questions about the robbery.

_____

_____

Student B
You are someone in the story—the doctor, a customer, a bank teller, or a policeman. Answer the TV interviewer's questions.

_____

_____

LISTENING TACTICS

1. In the following sentence we can put the stress in two different places. If we say it like this:

They went on **vacation** yesterday,

the most important information is _what_ happened. If we say it like this:

They went on vacation **yesterday**,

the most important information is _when_ something happened.

Decide if the speaker is emphasizing _what_ or _when_ something happened. Check the table below.

	What	When
1.	☐	☐
2.	☐	☐
3.	☐	☐
4.	☐	☐
5.	☐	☐
6.	☐	☐
7.	☐	☐

2. Listen to these sentences.

> *After lunch, the two presidents had a long discussion.*
> *Following the meeting, there was a dinner.*
> *Before the meeting, there was an interview for reporters.*

These sentences refer to things that happened at different times. Now listen to these sentences.

> *As the car drove up, the van drove away.*
> *While the bus was leaving, someone ran onto the road.*
> *During the trip, several passengers became ill.*

These sentences refer to things that happened at the same time. Now listen to the following sentences, and check *Different times* or *Same time*.

Different times	Same time
1. ☐	☐
2. ☐	☐
3. ☐	☐
4. ☐	☐
5. ☐	☐
6. ☐	☐
7. ☐	☐
8. ☐	☐
9. ☐	☐
10. ☐	☐

TRYING IT OUT

Look at these photographs from a newspaper.
Work out a story about each photograph, and write headlines.

1. _____

_____

2. _____

_____

3. _____

_____

4. _____

_____

Answers to Trying It Out, Unit 1, part b (page 6).

1. detective
2. nurse
3. architect